AIRCRAFT

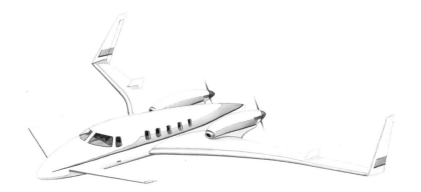

Max Fax:

AIRCRAFT

Also in this series:
Big Cats
Cars
Great Apes
Sharks
Space

Cover photograph: A Harrier, armed with missiles and bombs

Series editor: Cath Senker
Designer: Luke Herriott
Illustrator: Mark Bergin
Picture researchers: Gina Brown and Shelley Noronha
Language consultant: Wendy Cooling
Subject consultant: Ole Steen Hansen

First published in Great Britain in 2001
by Hodder Wayland, an imprint of
Hodder Children's Books
This paperback edition published in 2001

Reprinted in 2002

British Library Cataloguing in Publication Data
Malam, John
Aircraft. – (Max fax)
1. Airplanes – Juvenile literature
I. Title
629.1'3334
ISBN: 0 7502 34237

Printed in Hong Kong

Hodder Children's Books
A division of Hodder Headline Limited
338 Euston Road, London NW1 3BH

AIRCRAFT

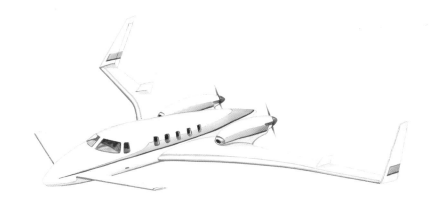

John Malam

HODDER
Wayland

an imprint of Hodder Children's Books

AIRCRAFT

SPREADING THEIR WINGS

A Boeing 747 carries up to 452 passengers.

Night and day, aircraft fly through the sky. From gigantic airliners to tiny gliders and powerful military planes, they are fantastic flying machines.

Passenger planes are for people. They take tourists to foreign countries, and business people to their meetings anywhere in the world. As more people choose to fly, bigger passenger planes are being made.

Flying can be fun. For some people it is a hobby. Small planes fly from airfield to airfield, microlights buzz over the ground,

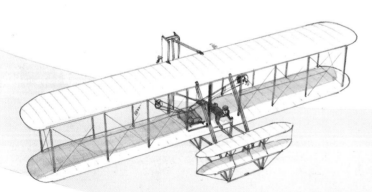

Wright brothers' 'Flyer' (1903): 0 passengers

Douglas DC3 (1930s): 28 passengers

An F-16 Fighting Falcon.

The world's air forces fly many different types of plane. Each has a special job to do. Some are fighters, some are transporters, and some are top-secret spy planes.

Cargo planes transport goods around the world. Some, like the odd-looking Airbus Beluga, are extra-large transporters, built to carry huge loads.

The Airbus A300-600T Beluga transporter.

What was the first engine-powered plane?

It was the 'Flyer', built in the USA by Orville and Wilbur Wright.

When did it first fly?

On 17 December 1903. This was the world's first flight of a craft that was heavier than air.

How long was the first flight?

Twelve seconds. The 'Flyer' flew for 37 metres.

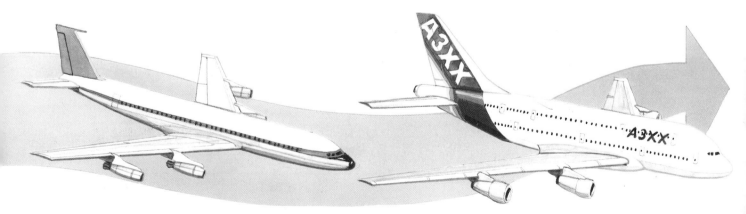

Boeing 707 (1950s): 189 passengers   *Airbus A3XX (2000s): 840 passengers*

NOSE TO TAIL

A plane is a complicated machine. But whether it is a sleek fighter or a bulky transporter, the basic design is the same.

The cockpit is a plane's command centre. It is a small cabin in the nose of the fuselage, where the pilot sits. Inside are the plane's flight controls.

The flight controls of a light aircraft.

A Beech Baron light aircraft

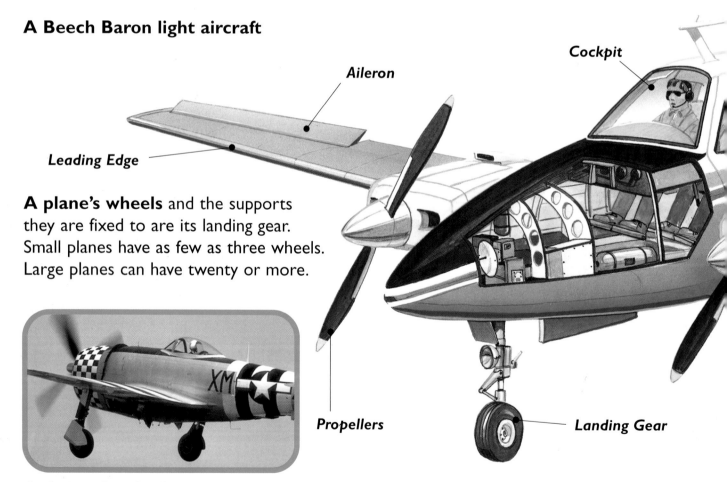

Aileron

Cockpit

Leading Edge

A plane's wheels and the supports they are fixed to are its landing gear. Small planes have as few as three wheels. Large planes can have twenty or more.

Propellers

Landing Gear

A plane with its landing gear down.

The fuselage is the body of a plane. It is where passengers sit and where cargo is stored. At the front are the flight crew. The wings are on the sides of the fuselage.

The plane's tail is at the far end of the fuselage. It helps to balance the plane when it is in the air.

Fin

Fuselage

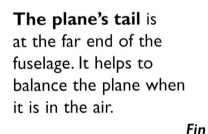

Elevator

Aileron

Fuel Tank

Engine

Which is the world's smallest piloted plane?

The *Bumble Bee II*, built in 1988. It has a wingspan of 1.67 m (5ft 6 in) and is 2.68 m (8ft 10 in) from nose to tail.

Which is the world's heaviest plane?

The Antonov An-225 *Mriya* (Dream), built to transport Russia's *Buran* space shuttle. It weighs 600 tonnes.

How many parts are in a Boeing 747?

4.5 million – 4 million are rivets!

FLYING FACTS

Flying boats – planes that could land and take off on water – were popular in the first half of the 20th century. The largest ever built was the *Spruce Goose*, a monster with a 97.5 m (320 ft) wingspan. Its only flight was in 1947, when it flew for a mile. Today, it is in a US museum.

FLYING HIGH

As a plane races down the runway, its pilot pulls back the control column. The wheels leave the ground and the plane soars into the sky.

A passenger plane's turbofan jet engine.

A plane stays in the air because its wings create a force called lift. Air flows faster over the wings' curved top than the flat bottom. This sucks the wings upwards.

Producing lift at different speeds

A passenger plane often has turbofan engines. Air enters at the front, and leaves the back at high speed. This makes thrust, the force that moves the plane forward.

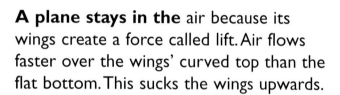

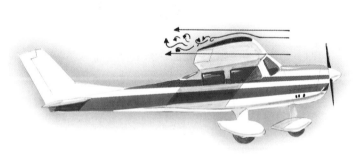

1. Low speed: wings are steeply angled into the air to produce enough lift.

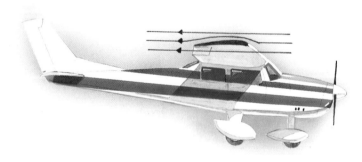

2. High speed: enough lift is produced with the wings at a lower angle.

A twin-engined Boeing 777 cruising above the clouds.

With flaps down, the plane lands at a lower speed.

How high does an airliner fly?

At cruising height, an airliner is about 10,000 m above the ground.

What fuel does an airliner use?

An airliner's jet engines use an aviation fuel called kerosene.

Do all planes have one pair of wings?

No. Biplanes have two pairs of wings. Triplanes have three pairs.

Movable panels steer a plane through the sky. Aileron panels on the wings make the plane go left or right. Elevator panels on the tailplane make it go up or down.

Planes follow set routes. They know which route to take because on-board computers pick up signals sent out by radio beacons on the ground.

13

PASSENGER PLANES

The Boeing 747-400, the world's largest airliner.

Passenger planes spend most of their lives in the air, flying people around the world. Some fly for long distances, while others make only short flights.

Boeing's 747-400 comes in four versions. The biggest is the Domestic. It takes 568 passengers on short flights. The Freighter version can carry up to 135 tonnes of cargo.

DID YOU KNOW?

* At any given moment, about 100,000 people are flying around the world in Boeing 747s.

* There are about 10,000 airliners in service today. By 2018 there will be 19,000.

* A Boeing 747 holds enough fuel to fill 3,000 family cars.

Concorde, the world's fastest airliner.

Concorde cruises at about 2,170 kph and is the world's only supersonic airliner. It flies from London to New York in three hours.

The De Havilland Dash 8 is a turboprop plane.

Some planes are designed for short-distance flights. The De Havilland Dash 8, built in Canada, flies up to 56 passengers on journeys of less than 1,500 km.

Inside a turboprop engine

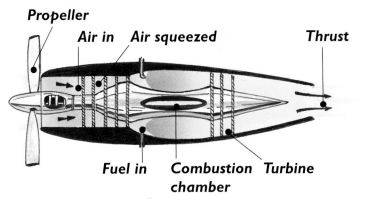

Propeller

Air in   Air squeezed

Thrust

Fuel in   Combustion   Turbine
chamber

In a turboprop engine, air and fuel burn inside a combustion chamber. As they burn they turn a turbine (a shaft which spins). As it spins, it turns the propeller round.

Are an airliner's tyres filled with air?

No. They're filled with nitrogen gas, which will not catch fire. Air-filled tyres could catch fire.

Where does an airliner store its fuel?

In its wings. Fuel tanks hold all the fuel needed for a flight.

How far can an airliner fly before refuelling?

The Boeing 777 can fly non-stop for 8,900 km.

MILITARY AIRCRAFT

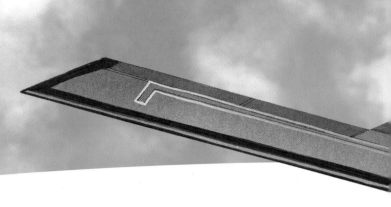

They're fast, they're mean, and they pack a powerful punch. They're fighters and bombers, the sharks of the skies. In wars they seek out and destroy the enemy. In peacetime they patrol from the air.

A military pilot learns to fly using a flight simulator on the ground. Then he or she flies a small two-seater jet called a combat trainer. The teacher is an experienced pilot.

There is a plane that does not need a runway. The Harrier is a Vertical Take-Off-and-Land (VTOL) fighter. It surprises the enemy by flying from clearings, like a bird.

How does stealth technology work?

Stealth planes are almost invisible to radar. Radar waves bounce off them, or are absorbed by them.

How much does a B-2 stealth bomber cost?

An incredible $2.2 billion (£1.5 billion) – the most expensive aircraft yet made.

What is the warload of a B-2 stealth bomber?

Up to 22,680 kg (50,000 lb) of bombs.

A Harrier lands on the deck of an aircraft carrier.

A B-2 stealth bomber releases a cruise missile.

The B-2 is a long-range stealth bomber armed with cruise missiles, mines, nuclear weapons, or laser-guided bombs. Only twenty of these giants have been built.

FLYING FACTS

Some warplanes, especially jet fighters, have triangular wings. They're called delta wings, after the Greek letter 'delta', which looks like a triangle. Delta wings let a plane fly easily through the sound barrier. Concorde and the Space Shuttle also have delta wings.

Not all military planes have a combat role. Some are reconnaissance planes, armed with cameras, not guns and bombs.

The Dassault Rafale, a modern delta-wing fighter built in France.

WHIRLYBIRDS

A Chinook can easily lift and carry a truck.

Helicopters are the best when it comes to moving a load, knocking out a tank, rescuing people at sea or checking on the traffic.

The Chinook is the load-lugger of the sky. This huge helicopter, with rotor blades at either end of its fuselage, can carry 55 troops – plus a truck beneath it!

The Apache is the supreme tank-busting chopper, armed with Hellfire and also Stinger, Starstreak or Sidewinder rockets. It's a fast-attack helicopter with a vital battlefield role.

How a helicopter flies

A lot of lift

Steep angle

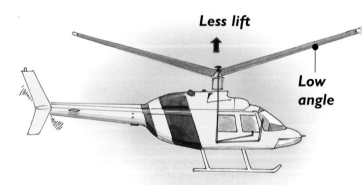

Less lift

Low angle

1. To go up, the pilot sets the rotor blades (these are like spinning wings) to a steep angle.

2. To come down, the pilot sets the rotor blades to a low angle. This makes less lift.

DID YOU KNOW?

* Leonardo da Vinci drew a helicopter design 500 years ago.

* The first helicopter flew in 1907. The flight lasted 20 seconds and the machine rose 2 m off the ground!

* In 1972 a helicopter rose to 12,442 m, the highest a helicopter has ever flown.

An air–sea rescue helicopter in action.

Many a shipwrecked sailor owes his life to a helicopter. Air–sea helicopters pluck people from the sea, then ferry them safely home to dry land.

Radio and TV stations use helicopters to spot traffic jams and the police use them to follow stolen cars. Some business people travel in them to their meetings.

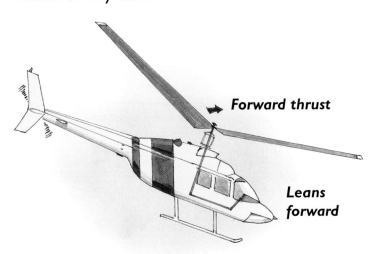

Forward thrust

Leans forward

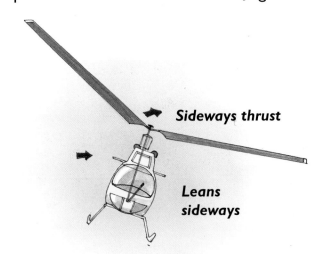

Sideways thrust

Leans sideways

3. To fly forwards, the pilot sets the rotors to lean down at the front. This makes forward thrust.

4. To fly sideways, the pilot sets the rotors to lean sideways. This makes sideways thrust.

PLANE FUN

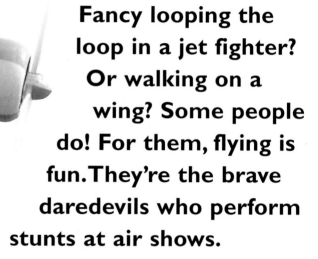

A wing-walker, balanced on the wing of a biplane.

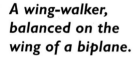

Fancy looping the loop in a jet fighter? Or walking on a wing? Some people do! For them, flying is fun. They're the brave daredevils who perform stunts at air shows.

If it flies, look for it at an air show. Military and civilian planes from around the world fly in for these events. It's a chance to see rare and unusual planes close-up.

Collecting old planes is a popular hobby. It doesn't matter what kind of planes they are. People have fun restoring them until they are in perfect flying order.

The Red Arrows display team in close formation, UK.

Flying upside-down is all in a day's work for the Northern Lights Aerobatic Team, USA.

For some people, having fun in a plane means flying a microlight. It's like a kite with a tiny motor fixed to it. It flies low and slow, and can land on a grassy airstrip.

Many air forces have display teams. Their planes perform aerobatic stunts. Brave pilots make the planes roll, spin, dive and climb. It's great to see them in action.

Pegasus microlight

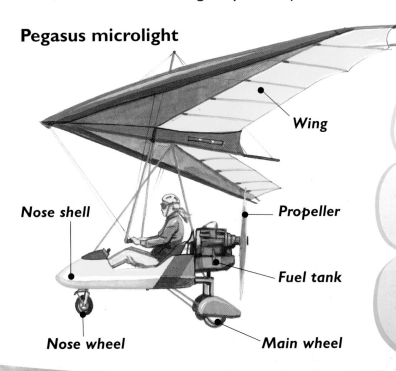

Wing

Nose shell

Propeller

Fuel tank

Nose wheel

Main wheel

DID YOU KNOW?

✱ Coloured smoke made by display planes is actually vapour from diesel fuel, coloured with dye.

✱ A microlight pilot steers the aircraft by shifting his or her body from side to side.

✱ Wing-walkers say: 'Never let go of what you've got until you've got hold of something else!'

AMAZING AIRCRAFT

There are some amazing aircraft, from floating gas bags to planes that can almost fly into space. They are extreme machines, built to test new ideas about flight.

The 1930s Graf Zeppelin airship.

Airships used to fly passengers around the world. These huge balloons, made of gas-filled bags, floated quietly through the air.

Experimental planes, known as 'X' planes, are built to test ideas. In the 1960s, the X-15 rocket plane tested high-altitude flight. It prepared the way for space flight.

X-15 launch

B-52 bomber

F-104 Star fighter

X-15 rocket plane

The X-15 rocket plane was launched from under the wing of a B-52. An F-104 chase plane flew with the X-15 to watch over it.

The F-117A Stealth Fighter is known as the 'Black Jet'.

Secretly built, the F-117A is one of the world's most advanced fighter planes. Lasers guide its missiles so that they hit the enemy right on target.

Unmanned Aerial Vehicles (UAVs) are small, strange-looking planes controlled by military operators on the ground. As they fly over battlefields, they spy on the enemy.

DID YOU KNOW?

✳ The first plane to fly faster than the speed of sound (1,195 kph) was the X-1, in 1947.

✳ You hear a 'boom' when a plane breaks the sound barrier.

✳ When Joseph Walker flew the X-15 to an altitude of 108 km, he was on the edge of space.

The Predator UAV gathers information about enemy ships and submarines.

FUTURE FLYERS

Planes have come a long way since their first fluttering flights. What can we say about their future? They'll be bigger and faster – and you'll probably be able to fly into space in one!

The F-22 Raptor is a fighter of the future.

Passenger planes of the future will be bigger than any planes now in the sky. Aircraft companies such as Boeing and Airbus are looking to build giant airliners.

Fighters, like the F-22, will have stealth features and superior flight handling. Their mission will be to control the skies on a first-look, first-shot, first-kill basis.

A computer image of an Airbus A3XX airliner. In future it will be called the A380.

Boeing V-22 Osprey tilt-rotor.

Tilt-rotors are already in service. Part helicopter, part plane, they are ideal for bringing people into city centres.

X-33, a re-usable Earth-to-space craft.

DID YOU KNOW?

✳ One version of the Airbus A380 is planned to carry 840 passengers.

✳ Companies are looking at building airships again. They will be smaller, faster and safer than the old ones.

✳ Large passenger planes will fly higher, where they will use less fuel in the thin atmosphere.

The X-33 might be the future for flights into space. It's designed as a Re-usable Launch Vehicle (RLV), and will launch vertically like a rocket but land horizontally like a plane.

AIRCRAFT QUIZ

Can you find the right answers to these questions? They can all be found somewhere in this book. Check your answers on page 29.

1. What is a plane's body called?
a The cockpit
b The fuselage
c The cabin

2. For how long did the Wright 'Flyer' stay in the air?
a 12 seconds
b 22 seconds
c 32 seconds

3. How many pairs of wings does a triplane have?
a 1
b 2
c 3

4. What is stored in an airliner's wings?
a Fuel
b Bombs
c Cargo

5. Which plane will fly into space?
a The X-1
b The X-15
c The X-33

6. Which fighter plane takes off like a bird?
a Hawk
b Harrier
c Hornet

7. What are Stingers and Sidewinders?
a Snakes
b Missiles
c Helicopters

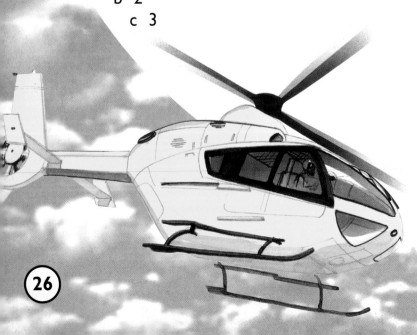

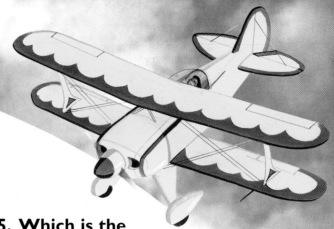

8. At low speed, a plane's wings are:
a Not angled in the air
b Slightly angled in the air
c Steeply angled in the air

9. What happened in 1903?
a The first helicopter flew
b The first airship flew
c The first plane flew

10. What does 'X' stand for in X-plane?
a Extreme
b Experimental
c Extra

11. A delta wing is what shape?
a Triangular
b Diamond-shaped
c Rectangular

12. What is a turbofan?
a A type of landing gear
b A type of cockpit
c A type of engine

13. The aileron panels make the plane:
a Go up or down
b Go left or right
c Go in to land

14. Which aircraft has rotors?
a A microlight
b A glider
c A helicopter

15. Which is the heaviest plane?
a Airbus Beluga
b Antonov An-225
c Boeing 777

16. What are an airliner's tyres filled with?
a Oxygen
b Carbon dioxide
c Nitrogen

17. Which plane is the Black Jet?
a The F-117A
b The F-22 Raptor
c The F-16 Fighting Falcon

18. Which is not a nickname for a helicopter?
a Whirlybird
b Spinner
c Chopper

GLOSSARY

ailerons Movable panels on the wings to make a plane go left or right.

airliner A large passenger aircraft.

altitude Height.

cockpit The front of a plane where the pilot sits.

delta wing A triangular-shaped wing.

elevators Movable panels on the tailplane to make a plane go up or down.

flight simulator A machine used on the ground to train pilots to fly.

fuselage The body section of a plane.

glider An aircraft without an engine that uses air currents to stay up in the air.

kerosene Aviation fuel for planes.

lift The force that lets a plane rise into the air.

microlight A tiny, lightweight plane with a small engine.

radio beacon A navigation device.

reconnaissance Looking at areas behind enemy lines.

rivets Nails or bolts for holding together metal plates.

RLV Re-usable Launch Vehicle. A plane that can fly into space, land, and be used again.

rotor The 'wings' of a helicopter.

stealth Technology that makes a plane invisible to radar-tracking equipment.

supersonic Faster than the speed of sound in air (332 m per second).

thrust The force that pushes an aircraft through the air.

tilt-rotor A plane with rotor blades and fixed wings.

turbofan A type of jet engine that has a fan to provide extra thrust.

turboprop A type of jet engine that has a spinning propeller.

UAV Unmanned Aerial Vehicle. A remote-controlled plane.

VTOL Vertical Take-Off-and-Land.

FINDING OUT MORE

Books

20th Century Inventions: Aircraft by Ole Steen Hansen (Hodder Wayland, 1997)

Eyewitness Guides: Flying Machine by Andrew Nahum (Dorling Kindersley, 1990)

Fighter Planes by Bill Gunston (Ticktock Publishing, 1999)

The Need for Speed: Aircraft by Chris Maynard (Franklin Watts, 1999)

Speedy Machines: Planes by Vic Parker (Belitha Press, 2000)

Supreme Machines: Aircraft by M. Battenield (Franklin Watts, 1999)

Ultimate Aircraft by Philip Jarrett (Dorling Kindersley, 2000)

Websites

Boeing:
www.boeing.com
Helicopters:
www.geocities.com/CapeCanaveral/
Launchpad/5249/index22.htm
Red Arrows Display Team:
www.deltaweb.co.uk/reds
X-planes:
www.dfrc.nasa.gov/History/x-planes.html

Places to visit

Brooklands Museum, Weybridge, Surrey (large collection of vintage planes)
Imperial War Museum, Duxford, Cambridgeshire (the UK's largest collection)
Heathrow Airport viewers' platform
International Helicopter Museum, Weston-super-Mare, Somerset (helicopters from around the world)
Manchester Airport viewers' platform
RAF Museum, Hendon, London
The Science Museum, London (many displays about flight and aircraft)
Shuttleworth Collection, Old Warden Aerodrome, Bedfordshire

Answers to quiz

1	b	7	b	13	b
2	a	8	c	14	c
3	c	9	c	15	b
4	a	10	b	16	c
5	c	11	a	17	a
6	b	12	c	18	b

INDEX

Page numbers in **bold** mean there is a picture on the page.

Picture acknowledgements

Boeing 14 (above); Ole Steen Hansen 8 (right), 12; The Plane Picture Company (all John M. Dibbs) *Cover*, 10 (above), 13 (above), 15, 20 (below); Quadrant (Mark Wagner) 8 (left), (Roger Ellis) 9 (above), (Jeremy Hoare) 13 (below), (Ian Press) 21, 22, (Erik Simonsen) 23 (below), 25; TRH (Daimler-Benz Aerospace) 9 (below), (E. Nevill) 10 (below), (Stuart H. Bourne) 14 (below), (McDonnell Douglas) 16, (F. Robineau) 17, (Boeing) 18, (Sikorsky) 19, (Boeing Stearman) 20 (above), (Lockheed) 23 (above), (Lockheed Martin) 24 (above), (British Aerospace) 24 (below).